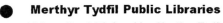

D0317561

To our grandson Cole, with love
—T.R.

IF I RAN THE DOG SHOW
A BANTAM BOOK 978 0 857 51358 8

Published in Great Britain by Bantam,
an imprint of Random House Children's Publishers UK
A Random House Group Company.

This edition published 2012

Based in part on *The Cat in the Hat Knows a Lot About That!* TV series.
© CITH Productions, Inc. (a subsidiary of Portfolio Entertainment, Inc.), and Red Hat Animation, Ltd.
(a subsidiary of Collingwood O'Hare Productions, Ltd.), 2010-2011.

Bantam Books are published by Random House Children's Publishers UK,
61–63 Uxbridge Road, London W5 5SA

Seussville.com
www.**randomhousechildrens**.co.uk

Addresses for companies within The Random House Group Limited can be found at:
www.randomhouse.co.uk/offices.htm

THE RANDOM HOUSE GROUP Limited Reg. No. 954009

A CIP catalogue record for this book is available from the British Library

Printed in China

If I Ran the
Dog Show

by Tish Rabe

illustrated by Aristides Ruiz and Joe Mathieu

BANTAM BOOKS

I'm the Cat in the Hat,
and today we will go
to the Short-Shaggy-Tail-Waggy
Super Dog Show!

Dogs are mammals like us,
and their senses are keen.
We will meet lots of dogs,
and you'll see what I mean.

Every dog is invited.
The tickets are free.
It's starting right now.
Grab a lead! Follow me!

There are millions of dogs,
and they live the world over.
Meet Plucky and Lucky
and Ruby and Rover.

There are big dogs and small dogs
and dogs in between,
in more shapes and sizes
than you've ever seen!

Dogs are loyal and true,
and they're eager to please.
They sniff everything –
people, rocks, grass and trees!

Dogs can do lots of things.
They like running and catching
and howling and prowling
and sniffing and scratching.

THE SHORT-SHAGGY-
SUPER

7

Here is the world's biggest build-a-dog puzzle. This part of a dog's face is known as the muzzle.

MUZZLE

STOP

NOSE

EAR

CREST

WITHERS

NECK

CHEST

SHOULDER

BRISKE

ELBOW

UPPER ARM

8

Now I'll show you the ears,
the withers, the crest,
the shoulder, the elbow,
the brisket, the chest.

LOIN

TAIL SET

Dogs have a thick pad and
four nails on each paw.
On each foreleg a fifth nail
is called a dewclaw.

9

Dogs' eyes can be golden,
dark brown, or light blue,
round or triangular
or almond-shaped, too.

Their heads can be long
and narrow like this collie's
or shorter and wider
like this French mastiff dog Molly's.

Their ears come in all shapes,
and I happen to know
erect ears stand up high
and pendant ears hang low.

Dogs' tails are all different.
Some are straight, and some bend.
A hook tail hangs down,
then curves up at the end.

Tails can be short, long, straight,
curly or plume.
Plucky wagged her long tail
when I walked in the room!

Tails help a dog balance.
Look out! There goes Rover!
His tail keeps him steady
so he won't fall over.

The tail muscles help
hold it higher or lower,
and help a dog wag
its tail faster or slower.

Dogs are carnivores,
which means they eat meat.
Their sharp teeth help make
the meat easy to eat.

I've studied dogs' teeth.
Now I've got it right.
When top teeth hang over,
it's called overbite.

When bottom teeth stick out
like this bulldog's teeth do,
it's called underbite.
(Other dogs have this, too.)

Fur helps keep dogs warm
and protects their skin.
Sara's thick fur keeps
her body heat in.

Would you like to meet
this nice dog named Shirley?
Her fur is quite long
and you see it is curly.

Some dogs' coats have patterns.
Look at Scratchy's back.
His coat has a pattern
of tan fur and black.

Some dogs you see
have loose folds in their coats.
Dewlaps are loose folds
up under their throats.

Sara was trained
and now understands
the words "sit,"

"stay,"

and "heel,"
which are spoken
commands.

Dogs may bark to tell you,
"Let's go for a walk!"
But barking is only
one way dogs can talk.

If a dog starts to growl or
has teeth that are bared,
that means she is angry.

Grrrrr...

If he whimpers, he's scared.

If a dog feels okay,
then its tail is upright.
If its tail's drooping down,
something might not be right.

DOG
TRE

Dogs are all different breeds.
You'll see in this book
just how very different
some breeds of dogs look.

Irish wolfhounds like Baxter
are the breed that is tallest.
Chihuahuas like Chico are
the breed that is smallest.

Purebreds have parents
the same breed as each other,
like these poodle puppies
with their father and mother.

This dog's name is Wendell.
He likes to do tricks.
What breed is Wendell?
This dog is a mix.

I have pictures right here
of his father and mother.
His father was one breed,
his mother another.

A mixed breed, or mutt,
I can safely say,
is the most common dog
in the U. S. of A.

21

German shepherds are brave
and have nerves that are steady.
For any emergency,
they're always ready.

Bloodhounds are so good
at tracking a scent,
if someone is lost they can
smell where he went.

Labradors like Rover
like to run, jump and swim.
Having fun with kids
is perfect for him.

Greyhounds have long legs,
and these dogs, I know,
can run fast and they're
always ready to *go*!

24

Some dogs have short legs,
like this basset hound.
When she moves around,
she is low to the ground.

Silky terriers like Scampi
have long hair that flows.
Sometimes this long hair
is held up
with bows.

Long hair like Scampi's
is called a head fall.
Chinese crested dogs
have almost no hair at all.

This dog's having puppies!
She's patiently waiting.
Dogs give birth about sixty-three
days after mating.

When she has her puppies,
she'll have more than one.
She could have ten or more
before she is done.

Puppies like to play.
They like snarling and biting.
They're not really angry.
They're only play-fighting.

26

Here is a poem
I wrote for these pages.
It's a poem about how
puppies grow up in stages.

I AM A PUPPY
by
the Cat in the Hat

I am one day old.
I can't hear and can't see.
But I can smell my mother.
I know she's near me.

I am three weeks old.
Now I start to explore.
What's this? It's a toy
I just found on the floor.

I am six weeks old.
My sister wants to play,
but she likes to bite
so I push her away.

I am eight weeks old.
There's a lot that I know.
I have a collar and lead
and I'm ready to go!

Now it is time for
the next presentation –
a "How Do Dogs See,
Hear and Smell?" demonstration.

Dogs have good vision.
Their keen sense of sight
helps them to see better
than people in dim light.

Dogs hear high-pitched sounds that people can't hear. Scratchy heard a mouse squeak and knew it was near.

TRASH

I blew this dog whistle and though I was near it, Lucky heard the whistle but I couldn't hear it.

Dogs' noses work well.
When Jack smells your clothes,
the smell goes to scent
receptors in his nose.

Then the olfactory nerve,
I would like to explain,
brings the smell from his nose
right up into his brain.

THE NOSE KNOWS

JACK

BRAIN

Whenever a dog smells
your clothes and you,
it knows where you've been
and what you've been up to!

HOT DOGS

Dogs can help people,
and here are a few
of the helpful things some dogs
can be trained to do.

DOGS ON THE JOB

This dog has been
trained as a guide.
When his owner goes out,
he is right at her side.

Therapy dogs bring
tail-wagging cheer.
People feel better when
these dogs are near.

They are specially trained,
so when they're invited,
they stay calm and friendly
and don't get excited.

Assistance dogs like Bob
can open up doors,
turn on lights, find lost keys
and pick things up from floors.

Sniffer dogs can find things
with their keen sense of smell.
If there's fruit in this suitcase,
this beagle can tell.

BEAGLE
BRIGADE

Search and rescue dogs
work to find people in trouble.
In an earthquake, they find
those who are trapped in the rubble.

Police dogs have badges.
Scout, as you can see,
is wearing his badge:
number 6183.

The dog show is over,
and I have a prize
for every dog here,
every colour and size.

Dogs live all around us,
and we've seen today
dogs live in our world
in their own special way.

When we walk in the door,
they come running to meet us.
Wet kisses and tail wags
are right there to greet us.

There are many things
that all these dogs can do,
but what they want most
is to spend time with you.

THE CAT IN THE HAT
Knows a Lot About That!™

The Garden of Seasons shows you everything about autumn and winter, summer and spring! With the Cat's friend Gardenia along for the fun there's year-round excitement for everyone!

ISBN 978-0-857-51115-7
PRICE £3.99

Are the colours the same in every rainbow? The Cat in the Hat knows just where to go to learn about that, and so very much more. Hop aboard! The next stop is Colour-galore!

ISBN 978-0-857-51059-4
PRICE £3.99